Original title:
Meaning: It's Probably in the Soup

Copyright © 2025 Creative Arts Management OÜ
All rights reserved.

Author: Levi Montgomery
ISBN HARDBACK: 978-1-80566-280-8
ISBN PAPERBACK: 978-1-80566-575-5

The Essence of the Ordinary

In the pot brews a tale, so round,
With carrots and dreams, blending sound.
A pinch of this, a dash of glee,
Life served hot, just wait and see.

Spoonful of chaos, a gulp of cheer,
Stirring the mix, we hold dear.
Simple things, they hold the key,
To tastes of joy, so wild and free.

Lessons from the Ladle

The ladle's wisdom flows with grace,
Sipping from the pot, we find our place.
Swirling in circles, laughter spins,
Flavor and folly, where joy begins.

Drip drop, we learn, it's quite absurd,
In every drop, a funny word.
Ladles share secrets, quite a few,
In soupy whispers, life's brew is true.

Mixing the Inexplicable

What's that smell? A curious blend,
Of spices and giggles, on which we depend.
A sprinkle of nonsense, a splash of fun,
In the steamy pot, our worries are done.

Chop chop, the veggies tell their tales,
Of past lives lived, like circus trails.
Dancing in broth, they take a leap,
Unraveling dreams, in textures deep.

Secret Recipes for Existence

A recipe's scribble, a messy hand,
With ingredients unknown, it's quite unplanned.
Mix in a chuckle, a fold of surprise,
Taste the absurd, as laughter flies.

Bubbles of wisdom simmer and rise,
In every dish, a hint of the skies.
So when in doubt, just reach for the stew,
For life's bubbling secrets await for you.

Matters of the Kettle

Oh kettle, bubbling with delight,
You hide the secrets, thick and tight.
With carrots dancing, peas in a row,
A symphony brews, from high to low.

Onions weep, while garlic sings,
With each new stir, joy it brings.
Is that a whisper from the thyme?
Or just my stomach, keeping time?

A splash of chaos, a sprinkle of cheer,
Each spoonful's laughter, oh so near.
Broth deepens like an old joke told,
As flavors mingle, a feast unfolds.

Flavors of Solitude

In solitude, the pot does hum,
With broth so rich, and flavors numb.
A dash of whimsy, a pinch of glee,
Taste the silence, just you and me.

The aromas swirl in playful chase,
With every simmer, a smiling face.
Carrots like comedians, peas will jest,
A solo act, but feels like the best.

By the window, I sit and stew,
Imagining laughter, both old and new.
A funny thing, this solo brew,
Yet somehow, it brings warmth to view.

Unwritten Ingredients

A recipe lost, in chaos thick,
I toss in laughter, and humor's trick.
What else to add? A pinch of grace,
And maybe a splash, of silly face.

The garlic's grinning, the broth's a tease,
The veggies all conspire to please.
Every guesswork leads to delight,
As steam rises softly, a comical sight.

With zest of life, and fun in the mix,
This pot of inspiration, full of tricks.
No rules to follow, just taste and try,
An unwritten secret, that makes you sigh.

Stirring Shadows

In shadows, I stir the broth so warm,
Each ingredient whispers, a subtle charm.
Onions giggle, as I lift the lid,
In this quiet kitchen, no secrets hid.

The spoon creates ripples, like laughter's song,
As flavors rumble, they can't be wrong.
The garlic dances, the salt takes a bow,
In this merry pot, joy is the vow.

So here's to the shadows, where soup is spun,
Where flavors unite, and laughter's fun.
In every sip, a little surprise,
These stirring shadows will always rise.

A Tapestry of Flavors

In a pot where spices dance,
A pinch of joy, take a chance.
Laughter bubbles, flavors mix,
Stir in some wild, add a few tricks.

Carrots giggle, onions cry,
Tomatoes blush as they pass by.
Seasoned dreams in yellow hues,
Who knew soup could be such news?

A broth of tales, a dash of cheer,
Sipping slowly, taste the year.
Each spoonful whispers a jest,
Gathered round, we're truly blessed.

So ladle love into each bowl,
It's laughter that stirs the soul.
With flavors dancing, all is right,
We feast together, pure delight.

Distilling Experience

From garden's edge to kitchen bright,
Chop and drop, what a sight!
Celery snaps, a crunchy sound,
In this pot, joy's unbound.

A sprinkle here, a twirl over there,
Taste like laughter, nothing to spare.
Old secrets in every stew,
The broth reveals what's truly true.

Stirred with care and a dash of wit,
Each taste bud knows it's a perfect fit.
Churning memories, seasoned bold,
In every sip, a story told.

So raise your spoon, let's dive deep,
In this richness, laughter leaps.
With every bite, we share the fun,
In this brew, we're all as one.

The Deep Flavor of Silence

A whisper floats in simmering heat,
Where silence reigns, flavors meet.
A quiet pot, a thoughtful brew,
In the calm, we find what's true.

Broth of dreams, a gentle hush,
In each bubble, ideas rush.
What's unspoken, depth distilled,
In this quiet, hearts are filled.

Flavor settles, then takes flight,
In the stillness, stars shine bright.
Each ingredient, a quiet flair,
In this moment, we simply share.

So sip the silence, taste the calm,
In the broth, we feel the balm.
For in the quiet, we discover,
The deepest flavors, like no other.

Recipes of the Heart

A dash of love, a sprinkle cheer,
In every recipe, hold it near.
A little patience, a lot of fun,
In mixing hearts, we're never done.

From simmering tales to seasoned feats,
Each flavor tells of love's sweet treats.
Gathered round the kitchen table,
In this space, we're all able.

Stir in kindness, let laughter rise,
In every bowl, see the surprise.
From different paths, we come alone,
But in this soup, we find our home.

So take a taste, let joy impart,
Together we feast, that's just the start.
With every bite and every cheer,
In these recipes, love is clear.

The Alchemy of Taste

In a pot where chaos brews,
Carrots swim with ample views.
A dash of spice, a pinch of jest,
Turns bland to grand, the flavor quest.

Bubbling pot, loud and proud,
Onions weep, join the crowd.
A ladle's dance, a swirling spree,
What's in the soup? A mystery!

Stirring the Unknown

Whisking dreams in a simmering might,
A rogue tomato joins the flight.
Silly herbs play hide and seek,
While garlic sneaks a kiss on cheek.

What's next? A noodle cheer?
Or a pepper's whispered sneer?
With every stir, the giggles grow,
A soup of secrets, what a show!

Crumbs of Reflection

On crusty bread, the laughter spreads,
A sprinkle of joy atop what's said.
Each bite, a chuckle, a savory tease,
Yet crumbs on the table aim to please.

Leftover thoughts that dance in my head,
Play hide and seek with the meals I've fed.
A bite too salty, a laugh too loud,
In this feast of minds, we're all quite proud!

Culinary Confessions

Confessions stirred with a spatula bright,
Spoonfuls of whimsy take flight at night.
Garlic's crunch, the secrets revealed,
Broth of giggles, full and unsealed.

A recipe scribbled on a napkin's face,
With hints of spice, a dash of grace.
Every slurp tells a tale so deep,
In culinary dreams, we laugh and leap!

The Taste of Truth

In a pot where thoughts combine,
Laughter simmers, bites divine.
A sprinkle of joy, a dash of cheer,
Stirring up wisdom, never fear.

With every taste, we find the fun,
Noodles of nonsense, all in one.
The broth of life, a quirky blend,
You'll find the truth, just follow the trend.

Between the Bubbles

Bubbles rise with happy sounds,
In this pot, silliness abounds.
A tickle of spice, a giggle or two,
Each pop reveals something new.

The surface dances, reflections bright,
What lies beneath? Let's take a bite!
Forks and spoons all join the play,
Between the bubbles, we lose our way.

Croutons of Insight

Crunchy bits on thoughts so soft,
Mirth and wisdom, they lift us aloft.
Each crouton a nugget, a crispy delight,
Chewing on lessons well into the night.

Chomping through silly, a tangle of wit,
Flavorful truths in each savory bit.
Sipping the broth, let laughter sweep,
Croutons of insight, in joy, we leap.

The Secret Recipe

A pinch of chaos, a dash of delight,
Stir it all up, and it's sure to ignite.
The secret's not hidden, it's there in the ladle,
Recipe for laughter, a whimsical fable.

Combine the bizarre, let your heart bloom,
In this funny dish, there's always room.
So taste with your senses, let smiles unfold,
In every good soup, there's a story to be told.

The Palette of Experience

A pot of red and a sprinkle of green,
Tastes like wisdom, if you know what I mean.
Ladle out laughter, let joy be the spice,
Life's just a stew; don't forget to think twice.

With carrots of hope and onions of dreams,
Simmer them slowly; it's not as it seems.
Stir in some giggles, a dash of delight,
Serve it up hot, and everything's right!

Gather your friends with a bowl in their hand,
Sharing the flavors, it's simply unplanned.
A recipe written in moments we share,
Tasting together, defeating despair.

So here's to the broth of the stories we tell,
Each spoonful mixed with a laugh or a yell.
A scrumptious concoction, where all are set free,
Life's quirky buffet, come savor with me!

Essence Stirred with Purpose

Caught in the broth of a bustling café,
Sipping absurdity, keep boredom at bay.
A dash of confusion, a sprinkle of zest,
Life's quirky flavors always at their best.

Cabbage of chaos, potatoes of fun,
Grabbing a spoon, then it's all said and done!
Stirring up moments; oh, what will we find?
A recipe scribbled, with laughter entwined.

Simultaneously serious, yet light as a breeze,
The more that you sip, the more you'll appease.
With broccoli wisdom, and garlic of grace,
Each bite is a journey; it's never a race.

So when you feel dull, and your thoughts seem askew,
Just whip up a pot; it's a magic brew.
Let flavors remind you of all that you've been,
Essences blended, where fun can begin!

Simmering with Clarity

In a pot of reflections, let flavors collide,
A waltz with uncertainty, take it in stride.
Simmer thoughts slowly, let ideas expand,
The broth of the wild, unpredictable hand.

Laughter is marked with a slice of lime,
Adding that giggle, it's tastefully prime.
With noodles of nonsense, and chunks of delight,
Each spoonful's potential; it's simply alright!

Chop down the seriousness, let joy reign supreme,
Season the chaos, sprinkle a dream.
Stir in some friendship, let savory flow,
Collecting the wisdom, see how it grows.

So grab your old ladle, and take a deep scoop,
Dive into the depths of this whimsical soup.
Plunge in with purpose, and serve it with flair,
Simmering life lessons, all seasoned with care!

A Taste for Subtlety

A pinch of this, and a whisper of that,
Taste the unspoken, where laughter is at.
A swirl of spices on a canvas so bright,
Each droplet a giggle, oh what a delight!

With a dollop of chaos, and a twist of fate,
Sometimes the simplest can captivate.
Soused in absurdities, crafty and shrewd,
Life's playful escapades, season the mood.

Chop time into chunks, don't boil it away,
Savor each second in a humorous way.
Sprinkle on kindness, let flavors entwine,
In a bowl of togetherness, everything's fine!

So sip on the stories, both subtle and bold,
A concoction of memories, waiting to be told.
For in every laugh, and in every woop,
We discover the secrets of life's funny soup!

Flavor of Existence

In a pot where dreams collide,
Bubbles pop, and giggles slide.
A sprinkle here, a dash of glee,
Life's a feast, come taste with me.

Forks and spoons in joyful dance,
Slurping noodles, take a chance.
With every sip, absurdity brews,
In each bowl, a chuckle ensues.

Stirring the Depths

In the broth, a mystery stews,
Laughter bubbles, what to choose?
Grab a ladle, dig in deep,
Jokes simmer while we eat.

Celery sways, a stalk of cheer,
Onions laugh, they shed a tear.
In this kitchen, life's a joke,
Stir the pot and hear it poke.

In the Broth of Life

A soup so rich, flavors collide,
With every sip, let worries slide.
Chunks of joy and herbs of play,
In this concoction, we'll be okay.

Pour the broth, it's time to feast,
From spicy tales to laughter's beast.
The spoon a wand, let's cast some cheer,
In the broth, we hold what's dear.

Carrots and Contemplation

Carrots whisper with a crunch,
Sweetness dances in a punch.
Jokes and veggies intertwine,
In each bite, the world's divine.

Celery stalks stand straight in line,
As laughter mixes, oh so fine.
With every taste, a brand new thought,
In this bowl, what joy we've sought.

Nourishment in the Nonsense

A spoonful of chaos, splashed in the pot,
Laughter spills over with each silly thought.
Carrots are giggling, the peas are quite proud,
In this wacky soup, let's gather a crowd.

Onion tears mixing with joy and despair,
Tomatoes are dancing without any care.
A ladle of whimsy, a pinch of surprise,
Who knew life's broth could come with such highs?

Celery sticks play peek-a-boo bliss,
Each bite serves a chuckle, you can't miss this.
Flavors combine in a festival feast,
Where nonsense is king, and worries are ceased.

So grab your big spoon, let's stir up the fun,
With laughter and soup, who could not be won!
In each silly sip, adventures await,
Nourishment's found in this wacky state.

Parsley and Paradox

In a bowl of absurdity, herbal delight,
Parsley and paradox dance through the night.
With flavors that tangle and twist in a swirl,
They ponder life's questions with a giggle and twirl.

Basil's debating, while thyme takes a nap,
Rosemary grins from her fragrant little lap.
"Are we just a garnish?" they question with glee,
"We're the stars of this dish!" shouts the tomato, with glee.

The broth starts to bubble with nonsense and rhyme,
Every spoonful's a riddle, deliciously prime.
Lentils chime in with their hearty old jokes,
A banquet of laughter for all the fine folks.

As they simmer and stew, a sauce to confound,
This salad of thoughts wraps us tight all around.
In every odd flavor, a truth hides inside,
Parsley and paradox, our joy and our guide.

Sipping on Epiphanies

With each little sip, an idea ignites,
Flavorful tidbits, like playful delights.
Broth full of jokes, it's served in a cup,
Sipping on wisdom as we gather up.

Carrots whisper secrets when warmed by the sun,
Zucchini's a philosopher, always has fun.
In bowls of reflection, the stories unfold,
Where laughter and meaning are hand in hand told.

"Why does a noodle feel lost in the stew?"
Well, it's searching for purpose beyond its true hue!
With every long slurp comes a burst of delight,
Who knew insights thrived in the taste of the light?

So raise your own chalice, let's toast to the zing!
In a soup full of giggles, there's room for the king.
Each mouthful a marvel, with mysteries sipped,
Epiphanies rise where silliness dripped.

Stir-Fried Reflections

In a wok of confusion, a stir-fry of thought,
Noodles collide with the wisdom they sought.
Each veggie a lesson, as vibrant as dreams,
With laughter as seasoning, the silliness beams.

Garlic's a sage, with a strong sense of flair,
While peppers debate if they're spicy or rare.
The mushrooms provide a soft cushion of grace,
In this pan full of folly, we're all in one space.

As steam rises high, so do giggles and cheers,
It's the taste of the moment that tickles our fears.
A splash of soy sauce adds a kick to the mix,
In this stir-fried delight, we're a blend of odd tricks.

When served on a plate, it's a banquet of smiles,
With each crunchy bite bringing joy for a while.
So whip up some chaos, let the flavors collide,
In stir-fried reflections, let laughter reside.

The Delicacies of Life

In a pot, all dreams collide,
Carrots dance, and onions slide.
With every stir, the giggles grow,
What's in the mix? We just don't know!

A sprinkle here, a dash of cheer,
Laughter bubbles, never fear.
Taste the whimsy, feel the grin,
Is that joy? Or just a spin?

Flavoring Our Journey

Life's a stew, not plain or bland,
Add a pinch of silly, and take a stand.
From broccoli forests to potato hills,
Adventure awaits with savory thrills.

Chop and stir, let spirits rise,
Unexpected flavors, a fun surprise.
With friends at the table, all cheers abound,
In this pot of chaos, joy is found.

Soup of Promises

In this broth, we cook our fates,
A spoonful of hope, and a few light spates.
Sipping secrets with every ladle,
Life's sweet nothings dance on the table.

Tantalizing tales from every bowl,
With noodles of laughter, that nourish the soul.
Promises simmer, all warm and neat,
Who knew wisdom tasted so sweet?

Brothy Melodies

As broth bubbles in a jazzy tune,
Each ingredient sings, a joyful croon.
Tomatoes twirl, while spices jive,
This whimsical pot is so alive!

Ladle out laughter, a sprinkle of fun,
In every sip, life's not done.
With each hearty gulp, we're lighter still,
Just like that soup, we're blessed with a thrill.

Whispers of the Spices

In the pot where secrets brew,
Garlic grins and onions coo.
Cumin chuckles, thyme plays tricks,
While bay leaves share their little quips.

A ballet of flavors, quite a show,
Bubbling laughter, watch it flow.
Salt looks on with a knowing smirk,
Pepper sneezes, what a perk!

Each pinch a riddle, each dash a tale,
Silly stories, they never pale.
In the kitchen, joy takes flight,
Where the spices dance, hearts feel light.

So take a taste, don't be shy,
From every pot, a laugh draws nigh.
A spoonful of fun is what you need,
As humor simmers, let it lead!

A Ladle's Wisdom

The ladle laughs, a curvy line,
Scooping dreams, both yours and mine.
In its belly, stories plop,
From veggie scraps, they never stop.

"Stir me gently," it does implore,
"Mix in the giggles, then add some more.
A dash of folly, a splash of cheer,
That's how you make the best dish here!"

In every slurp, a lesson blooms,
From spicy flares to quiet fumes.
So heed the ladle's clever call,
Grab a bowl; it's fun for all.

So slosh and sizzle, spill and play,
Ladle whispers cook up the day.
With laughter simmered, love will thrive,
In pots of joy, we feel alive!

The Essence of Simmering

On the stove, the pot gurgles loud,
A bubbling banquet, a feast for the crowd.
As flavors mingle, they tickle the air,
With every wee bubble, a joke is laid bare.

Tomatoes tumble and zucchini roll,
Dancing together, that's the goal!
Sometimes they clash, sometimes they blend,
A rocky romance, but all good friends.

Steam rises upwards, with whispers of cheer,
"Don't sizzle too fast; let love appear."
Patience, dear cook, don't rush the swirl,
Let the pot giggle, let flavors unfurl!

The essence is laughter, the aroma is fun,
In the heart of the kitchen, we've already won.
With each hearty spoonful, we celebrate life,
Through simmering tides, we conquer strife.

Ingredients of the Soul

In the pantry, we find our stash,
Each jar a memory, a happy flash.
Flour dust dances, sugar spins bright,
Together they mix, creating delight.

A sprinkle of kindness, a measure of glee,
The secret ingredient? Just wait and see!
Stir in some chaos, a dollop of cheer,
The soul's recipe, crystal clear.

Carrots with giggles, potatoes with flair,
Every bite savored, love hangs in the air.
The table's adorned, plates filled in rows,
For this feast of laughter, everyone knows!

From soup to soul, let flavors unite,
With humor and warmth, every dish feels right.
So gather around, share a great laugh,
For the best secret's in the heart's craft.

The Pot and the Perception

In the pot, ideas stew,
A pinch of nonsense, a dash or two.
Laughter bubbles, flavors blend,
What's real? Just pretend!

Stir the thoughts, let them race,
Every whim finds its place.
Slurp it down, hot and bold,
In this broth, stories told.

Garnished with a smile or two,
Take a sip, what will you do?
Floating thoughts, a funky crew,
Taste what's silly, taste what's true.

When the spoon dips, what's to be found?
A giggle here, a quirky sound.
In the mix, humor clinks,
Time to ponder, and time to drink!

Savory Sentiments

Chop the onions, add some cheer,
Tomatoes squish, never fear.
A splash of laughter, a jest or two,
Flip the pot, a hearty brew!

Carrots dance as they dive in,
Each flavor sings, a jesty grin.
Herbs and spices twist and twirl,
In the pot, emotions whirl.

Spoon of smiles added fast,
Once bland, now a taste of the past.
With every scoop, joy you'll lend,
A soup that laughs, a true godsend.

So, grab a bowl, come join the fun,
What's your flavor? Everyone!
From silly slurps to boisterous cheer,
In this concoction, we find our gear!

Aroma of Ambiguity

Steamy whispers fill the air,
What's the secret lurking there?
A whiff of chaos, a trace of glee,
In this pot, what might it be?

Sizzle and pop, a curious sound,
In the mix, oddities abound.
A dash of doubt, a splash of love,
Is it soup? A gift from above?

Flavor notes dance on my tongue,
Is it wisdom, or just a pun?
Each sniff invites a ticklish thought,
In this potion, all is caught.

So take a chance, embrace the whim,
Each dip, a story; each sip, a hymn.
With laughter, we brew, and stir, and play,
In the aroma, we find our way!

The Melting Pot of Thought

Waiter, bring a big ol' bowl,
Filled with quirks and humor's goal.
Slosh and splash, flavors collide,
In this pot, let's take a ride!

Feed your mind with each new bite,
What's for lunch? Pure delight!
Blend of laughter, dash of sage,
In this stew, we break the cage.

No recipe writes what's inside,
Just a spoonful of fun, worldwide.
Dabble joy, stir in some jest,
In this pot, we're at our best.

So grab a ladle, dish it out,
Every flavor prompts a shout.
In this melting pot, we find the fun,
Join the feast, let thoughts run!

The Enigma of the Pot

A bubbling brew sits on the heat,
With veggies dancing, oh what a treat.
Carrots whisper secrets, peas roll in glee,
What magic is brewing? Just wait and see.

The lid clinks twice, a mystery stirs,
Is that a potato? Or just wild whirs?
A sprinkle of spice, a dash of surprise,
Dinner's a puzzle, wear your best guise.

A spoon dips deep, the flavors collide,
Both sweetness and spice have nowhere to hide.
Who knows the recipe, who makes the rules?
In this happy pot, we're all just fools.

At last, we shall feast, the guests take their share,
With laughter and giggles floating in air.
Each bowl tells a story, every sip sings,
In the end, it's all soup and what joy it brings!

Inviting Mystery to Dinner

The table is set with a curious flair,
With bowls full of colors, swirling in air.
What's on the menu? An enigma, it's true,
Invite your own guess; it's up to you!

Do we have noodles or is it a stew?
A fortune teller's job, what will you chew?
The bread rolls are giggling, the salad's in shock,
Mysteries abound with every tick-tock.

A pinch of this, a sprinkle of that,
Who knew this dinner would be such a riddle?
Crusty bread whispers, 'What's hiding inside?'
Only the brave dare open with pride.

Open your heart to the whims of the feast,
Each flavor a jest, at the very least.
As laughter erupts and stories unspool,
This meal is a puzzle—let's break every rule!

Under the Veil of Ingredients

Under a veil of spices and cream,
Lies a concoction, or so it would seem.
Is that a cinnamon stick on a spree?
Or just another spoonful of mystery?

Chopped onions giggle, embracing the heat,
Potatoes pirouette, oh, what a feat!
The garlic plays coy, sliding across the pan,
While secretive sauces plot, as they can.

A swirl of the ladle brings laughter and zest,
Each bite is a puzzle, a quirky quest.
In the depths of the pot, odd flavors unite,
Creating a dish that's a comic delight.

So gather your friends, bring your plate wide,
What's lurking in soup? Let's take it in stride.
A chorus of flavors sings loud and clear,
Under this veil, let's feast without fear!

Whims of the Whisk

A whisk starts to dance with a jubilant flair,
Eggs tumble and splash, flying everywhere.
Did it just make a mess or art with a twist?
Culinary antics I cannot resist!

With a flick and a swirl, do I add some more?
The butter laughs loudly, it knows what's in store.
Is this a grand cake or just wishful thinking?
The eggs and the cream continue their linking.

Oh, sugar, dear sugar, pour in with delight,
We'll whip this confusion until it's just right.
The bowl may be crazy, but that's half of the fun,
In the land of the whisk, we're never outdone.

So let's raise our forks, it's a festive parade,
Through whisked-up wonders, let's laugh and invade.
Each ingredient's humor brings giggles galore,
In the whims of the whisk, there's always much more!

Savoring Life's Ingredients

In the pot of every day,
We toss in joy and strife.
A sprinkle here, a dash of cheer,
Stir it well, that's life!

Add a pinch of mischief,
A dollop of surprise.
Each spoonful tells a tale,
With laughter in the guise.

Mixing thoughts like spices,
Taste the moments bold.
Simmer down your worries,
Let the warmth unfold.

Each flavor packs a lesson,
With every ladle thrown.
Savor life's big banquet,
Find joy in the unknown!

A Taste of Discovery

With each bite a mystery,
Adventure on the plate.
Soup of life, oh what fun,
Each slurp a twist of fate!

Broccoli and laughter,
Carrots bright and wild.
If life throws in some onions,
Cry joy, my inner child!

The simmer brings reflection,
The heat ignites a spark.
A sprinkle of nutmeg,
Turns the mundane to art.

Caution: flavor explosion,
A quest for taste anew!
With every spoon we dive deep,
Into this broth so true!

Ephemeral Ingredients

Life's a broth that bubbles,
Full of fleeting spice.
Grab the moments quickly,
For they're seldom twice!

Chopped dreams and diced hopes,
Stir together with flair.
Each taste is short and sweet,
A potpourri to share.

Herbs of laughter sprinkle,
As memories collide.
In the kitchen of our hearts,
Let the flavors guide.

So ladle out a fortune,
In every broth you blend.
Life's soup is rich and funny,
Find joy around the bend!

Beneath the Broth Lies Wisdom

Beneath the bubbling surface,
Secrets simmer low.
Each spoonful hides a lesson,
In the broth we know!

Whisk away the worries,
Let the flavors merge.
In the chaos there's a rhythm,
Join the joyous surge!

From garlic to the ginger,
Every taste's a clue.
Life's recipe is funny,
Serve it warm and new!

So ladle up the laughter,
Garnish with a smile.
In the broth of our existence,
Let's savor for a while!

Aroma of Understanding

In a bubbling pot, secrets stew,
Each whiff a hint of something new.
Onion tears, a dash of cheer,
Laughter rises, season it here.

A sprinkle of chaos, flavors collide,
Taste a tickle, a joyous ride.
Sipping slowly, we share our tales,
In this broth, friendship never fails.

Gossip mingles with spice and zest,
Each slurp a giggle, we're truly blessed.
Croutons of humor float on top,
With every bite, we'll never stop.

Aroma dances, tickle your nose,
Every noodle, a story grows.
In this kitchen where dreams are whipped,
Understanding brews, and hearts are tripped.

The Pot of Curiosity

In a cauldron big where wonders bloom,
A dash of wit brings life to the room.
What's simmering now? A riddle or two,
A pinch of nonsense to stir up the brew.

Ladle laughter from the pot's warm head,
Each scoop reveals what's left unsaid.
Peeking inside, we giggle and grin,
What else is hiding? Let the fun begin!

With every scoop, questions arise,
Where do the pickles plot their surprise?
As we stir the stories, absurdly droll,
In this jiggling broth, we find our role.

Curiosity bubbles, a savory quest,
Guessing the flavors, we're truly blessed.
In the pot of quirks, we each play our part,
It's a tasty adventure that warms the heart.

Spoons of Insight

With a silver spoon, we dip our dreams,
Swirling wonders in whimsical themes.
Each scoop reveals, both big and small,
The truths we've gathered, a feast for all.

Soup's on the table, ladles in hand,
Gather around, it's a whimsical band.
From broth to baguette, we munch and muse,
In this delightful dish, we'll never lose.

Broccoli whispers to carrots nearby,
"Are we just veggies, or do we fly?"
With every spoonful, our ideas sprout,
In our pot of knowledge, we twist and shout.

So lift your spoons to the skies above,
Taste the stories and serve up love.
In the slosh of our soup, insights appear,
A banquet of fun that draws us near!

Steeping in Stories

In a teapot bright, stories brew,
Each steeping tale, a sip of hue.
A dash of laughter, a sprinkle of cheer,
With every cup, the world feels near.

Tea leaves whisper what we can't see,
Swirling in warmth, wild and free.
Take a sip and let it unfold,
In these rich brews, our hearts turn bold.

With cookies and crumpets, we share our jest,
Every hearty laugh is a savory quest.
As tales tumble forth, we toast to delight,
In this steeping process, everything's right.

So let's pour our hearts, in friendship we sip,
From brilliance of dusk, to joy of the trip.
In the warmth of our kettle, stories do rise,
As we steep in good humor, under wide skies.

The Essence Unseen

In the pot, a mystery brews,
Lurking flavors, some old, some new.
A dash of giggles, a sprinkle of cheer,
What's not in the recipe may just appear.

Slurping softly, a taste for the brave,
Each sip brings laughter, memories save.
Unexpected twists in every bowl,
Who knew soup could awaken the soul?

Ingredients clash in a dance so absurd,
Why'd the noodle join? Haven't you heard?
With a wink and a nod, they swirl and they spin,
The broth has a secret; it's crazily thin.

So grab your spoon, partake in the fun,
With each little taste, a new life begun.
What's lost in the kitchen is found in the sip,
Is it truly the soup? Or the laugh on the trip?

Broth and Belief

There's comfort in steaming, a warm cozy bay,
Where spoons stir the doubts, but they just float away.
What is faith made of? A hint or a spice?
In each bubbling broth, the truth may suffice.

Carrots and onions, they gather with zest,
Singing the song of the culinary quest.
Relishing moments, garnished with cheer,
A belief in the broth erases the fear.

The world's full of flavors, both bitter and sweet,
And in every good slurp, you'll find something neat.
Just mince and just chop, with jubilation in sight,
Who knew that a broth could birth such delight?

So here's to the soup, our fondest delight,
In the heart of the kitchen, it's always just right.
Under the lid, all secrets run deep,
Pour one for the dreamers, a hug we can keep.

Savoring the Unsaid

A pot full of chatter, flavors collide,
What's said with a spoon transcends what's inside.
A silent exchange with each awkward slurp,
In the broth, unspoken truths twist and curd.

Swirl of the ladle, gentle and slow,
Reveals hidden secrets, more than we know.
What's missed in the banter, found deep in the stew,
Is laughter in chunks and a giggle or two.

With noodles like whispers, they twist and they bend,
Encouraging joy in the taste that won't end.
Each bowl holds a promise, a wink and a grin,
In savoring silence, true friendships begin.

So slurp with abandon, let flavors unite,
In this chaotic kitchen, everything's right.
What's unsaid is a dance, a delicate sip,
In every good recipe, there's friendship's little trip.

A Pinch of Perspective

A sprinkle of this, a dash of that,
What's not in the pot can still give a chat.
In the swirl of the soup, life's lessons appear,
A spicy surprise can brighten your year.

With every good scoop, there's something to glean,
A view from the spoon can change what you mean.
Tomatoes like gems, each one tells a tale,
The broth holds the strength when the day starts to pale.

So take a big gulp, let the chaos unfold,
There's magic in soup that never gets old.
For in the light steam, perceptions can shift,
A pinch of perspective can be quite the gift.

Embrace the unknown, let your taste buds run free,
In laughter and flavor, find what's meant to be.
In every warm bowl, there's a world of delight,
A recipe's art: it's amusingly right!

The Brew of Uncertainty

In a pot where thoughts collide,
Ingredients of doubt reside.
A sprinkle of worry, a pinch of cheer,
Simmering slowly, what's cooking here?

A ladle of laughter, a dash of surprise,
Frothy bubbles rise to the skies.
What flavor emerges? It's hard to say,
But everyone's hungry at the end of the day.

Stirred by the hands of fate and chance,
We swirl and simmer, we jig and dance.
So lift up your spoon, take a curious taste,
In this bubbling broth, there's no room for haste.

Garnished with joy and a hint of absurd,
Every sip is strange, each slurp is unheard.
On this wild journey, we must not lose hope,
In the pot of confusion, we learn how to cope.

The Soul's Simmering.

In the depths of a cauldron, thoughts twirl around,
With spices of wisdom silently found.
Boiling emotions, a humorous sight,
In the stew of existence, we drink day and night.

A slice of bliss and a dash of dread,
Mix them together and hear what's said.
Stir in some giggles, let worries dissolve,
In this combo of chaos, all problems evolve.

A pinch of confusion, a scoop of delight,
Crafting a banquet under the moonlight.
Cooked to perfection, served straight from the heart,
In the pot of the soul, we're all a small part.

So who really knows what this recipe makes?
All we can do is enjoy what it takes.
With each bumble and stumble, we find out what's true,
In the laughter of life, secrets simmer anew.

Stirring Whispers

Whispers float in the air like steam,
What's bubbling up? Is it a dream?
A spoonful of humor, just right on cue,
In this blend of chaos, everyone's due!

Seasoned with stories from far and wide,
Mixing old tales with a splash of pride.
The aroma is funky, the texture a blast,
Looking back at the moments we wished would last.

With every stir, a chuckle ignites,
What's hidden within? A joy that excites.
In the pot of our lives, we gather and share,
Stirring whispers of laughter, floating in the air.

So ladle out love with each quirky bite,
In this soup of our souls, everything's bright.
Let's feast on the whimsy, the joy that we find,
As the soup of existence warms body and mind.

A Dash of Understanding

Measure the moments in a quirky bowl,
Add a splash of wisdom to nourish the soul.
Chop up the laughter, toss in the fun,
With a stir of confusion, it's all come undone!

A sprinkle of kindness, a generous scoop,
Swirling together in this vibrant soup.
What's the recipe for living this way?
Just laugh with your heart, come what may!

With each bubbling pot, we learn as we grow,
A dash of understanding helps laughter flow.
So pour out your heart, let it marinate deep,
In the flavors of friendship, memories we keep.

Let's dive into soup that's steaming and rich,
With each goofy morsel, we discover a hitch.
In the feast of our quirks, there's no need to fuss,
With a hearty mix of love, it's delicious to us!

Embracing Flavorful Paradoxes

In a pot, all things collide,
Carrots chat with beans, side by side.
Tomatoes flip a funny tale,
While spices dance, they never fail.

A broccoli crown takes the lead,
Garlic whispers, 'This is the seed.'
Onion's tears are a happy song,
Stirring the chaos, it won't be long.

Cabbage joins with a haughty grace,
While peas giggle, a merry race.
Each flavor's jester in this show,
As laughter bubbles, oh what a glow!

So grab your spoon and take a dive,
In this broth, we're all alive.
Life's absurdity in every scoop,
Embrace the fun, join the soup troop!

The Quench of Questions

What's that flavor, oh so asks?
Is it joy or secret tasks?
A pinch of doubt, perhaps a dash,
Makes every slurp a silly clash.

In this bowl, curiosity brews,
With hearty doubts and playful clues.
Chop and stir, confusion reigns,
Yet laughter fills all the mundane pains.

With a ladle full of whimsy too,
What's the answer? 'Just chew and stew!'
Each gulp a riddle wrapped in cheer,
A soup that quells all doubt and fear.

So savor each swirl, each twist,
In flavors, questions can't be missed.
Grab a friend, make it a game,
In every sip, there's joy to claim!

A Broth of Being

Stir the pot, what's this delight?
Wandering flavors, a curious sight.
Zucchini jokes with the old, gray sage,
A broth of being, unfolds the page.

With each bubble, wisdom brews,
In this mix, life's essence ensues.
Chop the veggies, slice the doubt,
In a world of taste, we twist about.

Potatoes ponder, 'What's the key?'
While thyme chortles, 'Just let it be!'
Pour some laughter, a splash of fate,
In this bowl, our dreams await.

So lift your cup to the quirky blend,
Each slurp a message, twist around the bend.
In every layer, there's laughter's song,
In the broth of being, where we all belong!

Whispers of the Whisk

Whisk it good, let's spin a tale,
Of lazy cooks who set sail.
A dash of this, a sprinkle there,
In each swirl, laughter fills the air.

Onions giggle, they flip and flop,
As herbs come in, they never stop.
Come join the mix, it's quite the scene,
Whisking dreams, both funny and keen.

Broths bubbling, secrets fly,
What's this potion? Oh my, oh my!
Each ingredient carries a quirky vibe,
In this kitchen, smiles must imbibe.

So grab your whisk, let's start the fun,
Cooking together, we're never done.
In the hum of the kitchen, joy does persist,
With laughter and love, we can't resist!

The Depths of Flavor

In the pot a strange mix brews,
A pinch of chaos, a dash of blues.
Noodles dance with peas and meat,
What's in there? An oddball treat!

Spoon in hand, I take a dive,
Each bite makes my taste buds jive.
Tomatoes giggle, garlic sneezes,
In this broth, joy never ceases.

Carrots swim while onions play,
Is this gourmet? I can't say!
Simmered secrets, oh what fun,
My kitchen's where the laughs are spun.

From flavors bright, a tale unfolds,
In every slurp, a joke retold.
Beneath the bubbles, joy's alight,
In soup's embrace, the world feels right.

Recipes from the Heart

In a bowl, emotions blend,
Spices whisper, sentiments extend.
A dash of humor, a sprinkle of cheer,
Mom's recipe calls, cannot steer clear.

Chop the onions, try not to weep,
The secrets they hold, oh, oh so deep!
Stir in love, that's the secret part,
You'll find the treasure within your heart.

Laughter bubbles with each clink of the spoon,
Potatoes giggle, they're quite the cartoon.
A recipe passed down, a joyful charm,
In this kitchen, there's no harm.

Gather round, let the feasting commence,
Each bowl tells a tale, stricken with suspense.
From heart to plate, a tapestry bright,
In every bite, day dreams take flight.

Whirlwind of Spices

Whirling, swirling in the pot,
Garlic and ginger like a dance, a plot.
Cumin twirls with coriander's glee,
A flavor fiesta, do you wanna join me?

The chili flakes break out in song,
In the kitchen, we can't go wrong.
Paprika plays its trumpet loud,
Inviting all to join the crowd.

Dance of the herbs, in a fragrant rush,
Basil winks, while thyme turns to hush.
Oregano spins, a whimsical kick,
In this whirlwind, time goes quick.

At the end of the day, in bowls we collide,
With giggles and flavors, we all take a ride.
Savour the stories from spice to soup,
In this crazy kitchen, we all find our group.

Kettle of Contemplation

In my kettle, thoughts bubble high,
Ideas simmer, like clouds in the sky.
A pinch of insight, a spoonful of jest,
What's cooking today? It's anyone's guess!

Water's churning, pondering out loud,
Floating ideas, under a fluffy cloud.
Broth of reflections, swirling around,
In this kettle, what wisdom is found?

Toss in a notion, let it steep well,
Each concept brews, with a chiming bell.
Add a splash of laughter for zest,
In this bubbling pot, I feel so blessed.

So here's to the kettle, my thought-filled friend,
Pouring out wonders that never quite end.
In every sip, a giggle appears,
In this hearty brew, we conquer our fears.

Sizzling Epiphanies

A ladle in hand, I stir with glee,
Thoughts bubble up, wild as can be.
Carrots dance, peas take a dive,
Repurposed dreams, now come alive.

Onions lend wisdom, their tears make me wise,
Garlic confessions, no need for disguise.
Each broth I concoct, a lesson anew,
Who knew soup could hold so much to pursue?

Potatoes are heavy with dreams yet unmade,
While broccoli's laughter helps fears to evade.
A pinch of salt, and the spice starts to talk,
In this bubbling cauldron, new ideas unlock.

Ladle out joy, let the silliness flow,
In each hearty spoonful, there's always a show.
From a simple broth to profound realization,
Who knew that soup could spark such sensation?

The Collected Tastes

In a big pot, emotions collide,
Each ingredient plays, nowhere to hide.
Tomatoes chuckle, laughing with glee,
While peppers jive, full of esprit.

Stirring the pot, we gather our teams,
A flavor brigade, fulfilling our dreams.
The splash of the broth, a delightful surprise,
Awakening giggles and squinting our eyes.

Cilantro's bold kick, it adds to the fun,
With a zest and a zip, it dances, it runs.
Every bite pulls threads, connecting us tight,
In every spoonful, our souls take flight.

So gather 'round, share your bowlfuls of cheer,
In this melting pot magic, there's nothing to fear.
With laughter and flavors, together we'll play,
In the grand collective, we find our way!

Spices of Connection

A dash of this, a sprinkle of that,
Spices unite, imagine the chat!
Cumin and curry share secrets untold,
While paprika brings warmth, not just spice, but bold.

Chili flakes giggle, they spark up the heat,
Bringing zesty tales, can't be beat.
Basil giggles softly, gentle and sweet,
They share whispers of love in this savory treat.

In this grand fusion, we mingle and blend,
Laughter erupts, the good vibes ascend.
A sprinkle of humor, a twist of the spoon,
Creating connections, we sing a light tune.

So here in this kitchen, bond over the pot,
With a splash and a dash, now trouble is not.
Together we laugh, with flavors so bright,
In spices of joy, everything feels right!

What Simmering Reveals

As the broth bubbles slow, secrets arise,
A savory mystery beneath cloudy skies.
Grains float above, like hopes in a dream,
Each simmering thought, crafting a theme.

A bay leaf's whisper, a tale from the past,
While potatoes ponder, how long will this last?
Carrots hold stories, of sweetness and light,
In this bubbling science, it feels just right.

Turn down the heat, watch the flavors embrace,
Transforming the mundane into a grand chase.
Every stir brings laughter, a lesson unfolds,
In simmering silence, life's truths are retold.

So ladle the warmth, let the taste buds explore,
In this pot of wonders, there's always much more.
Through the laughter and broth, together we see,
What simmering yields, is pure comedy!

Lifting the Lid on Truth

In the pot, secrets stew,
A dash of laughter, a hint of blue.
Spoons clink like bells in the night,
What's cooking? Oh, what a sight!

A pinch of doubt, a sprinkle of cheer,
What's in this mix? Let's draw near!
They say it's wisdom; I just smell spice,
Don't you dare take that advice!

The bubbles rise like thoughts in my head,
With every swirl, new doubts are fed.
So lift that lid and take a peek,
Truth hiding beneath, it's kinda cheek!

What's that flavor? It's hard to tell,
Might be a tale or just a spell.
We laugh and taste, and then we cry,
For in the soup, truths often lie!

The Flavor of Existence

Life's a broth, simmering slow,
With spices that tickle, and some that glow.
Add a dash of joy for extra zest,
Savor the flavors, that's our quest!

How much is enough? Just a pinch,
Mix in the laughter and do a clinch.
Sour notes come, but sweet ones stay,
Stirring up drama along the way!

Some days are salty, others are sweet,
What's in this bowl? A curious treat.
Take a big gulp, let it swirl in your mind,
In the soup of life, what will you find?

Taste the moments that bubble and brew,
Nothing is bland, every flavor's true.
So lift your spoon and give a cheer,
For the flavor of life's always near!

Nourished by Mysteries

In the kitchen of fate, secrets blend,
Whisked in silence, around each bend.
The simmering pot holds what we seek,
Each ladle full, each giggle unique.

What's the recipe? Who could know?
A swirl of joy, with hints of woe.
Whip up the chaos, serve it right,
With nachos on the side, a tasty bite!

The stew thickens with tales untold,
Mushed up dreams left out in the cold.
Grab a crouton of hope, take a sip,
In this crazy broth, let your spirit flip!

A sprinkle of wonder, a dash of fright,
Eating our questions under moonlight.
In each spoonful, mysteries bloom,
So nourish your soul with that flavorful gloom!

The Soul's Recipe

What's in the pot? Just give it a stir,
A splash of mystery, that's for sure!
A cup of giggles, a dollop of doubt,
Whisked all together, let laughter sprout!

The ingredients list is wildly long,
With quirks that hum a humbly song.
Chop up the worries, simmer the care,
Dust off the darkness and toss it in there!

Blend the nonsense with joyful screams,
Season with friendship, or so it seems.
With every scoop, our spirits rise,
In the soup of life, see the surprise!

So fill your bowl, don't be shy,
Taste the adventure as you pass by.
The recipe's odd, but oh so fun,
In each delicious drop, we're all one!

Reflective Relish

A ladle dips, oh what a sight,
In a pot of chaos, day and night.
Where carrots dance and peas do sing,
Mysteries bloom in every fling.

A splash of thyme, a dash of cheer,
What is the truth? It's not so clear.
A meatball whispers, a noodle sighs,
Is wisdom hiding beneath the skies?

In every swirl, a joke is told,
Of stew and secrets, brave and bold.
The spoon's a guide, a funny chime,
What's in this dish? A riddle sublime!

Riddles in a Cup

In a steaming cup, the answers brew,
With spices twirling, old and new.
The cabbage giggles, the broth has nerve,
What is the secret? Let's observe!

Potatoes ponder, while onions cry,
For every sip, a chuckle is nigh.
The broth declares, with humor rife,
Each bowl contains a sliver of life.

A sprinkle of laugh, a dash of fun,
What's hidden deep, can't be outrun.
In every taste, a paradox waits,
Ladle out laughter, it satiates!

The Flavorful Inquiry

A pot of colors, bright and bold,
Each ingredient has a story to be told.
The garlic whispers, the broth feels proud,
What's hidden beneath, in a lively crowd?

Tomatoes twinkle, artichokes sway,
Is life just soup in disarray?
Chickpeas chuckle, in their soft mush,
Unravel the secrets, in a great rush!

Not just a meal, but wisdom's delight,
In every spoonful, a curious bite.
So dip your ladle, take a good look,
It's a flavorful tale, in the cook's book!

Cooking Up Questions

The pot bubbles up with mischief and cheer,
Got questions to ponder? Take a seat near!
With each little splash, a giggle unfolds,
Beneath all the spices, life's humor beholds.

What's in the mix? A splash of jest,
In every ingredient, a quirky quest.
The noodles twirl, the broth starts to clap,
Questions in soup, let's map the gap!

As peppers debate, and carrots unite,
In this quirky kitchen, all feels right.
For every ladle, there's wisdom to sip,
A tasty delight in each funny quip!

The Unknown in the Melange

In a pot where flavors collide,
Mysteries bubble with pride.
Who knows what's lurking inside?
A rubber chicken? A potato tried.

Broth so thick, with secrets to share,
A sprinkle of laughter hangs in the air.
Beneath the surface, a joke may lay,
A comic twist in the soup buffet.

The Gathering in the Bowl

Gather 'round in the big, wide bowl,
Each ingredient plays its role.
Carrots and peas, all jolly and bright,
They dance together, a wacky sight.

The broth grins, full of whimsy and spice,
Turning up flavors both naughty and nice.
"Join us, dear friend!" the noodles cheer,
While broccoli whispers, "I'm still here!"

A Pinch of Realizations

With a dash of salt and a pinch of fun,
Stirring the pot till the laughter's begun.
Every spoonful brings a new surprise,
What's this? A breadcrumb with sparkling eyes!

Tomatoes giggle, "We're in this too!"
"Just think of the tales," the cabbage coos true.
A napkin on the side chuckles fate,
When dinner is served, let's celebrate!

Craving What's Beneath

Beneath the layers, adventures await,
The wild and the wacky, they congregate.
One ladle pulls stories from depths unknown,
Where strange flavors and bad puns are grown.

A garlic clove whispers secrets untold,
"Get ready for laughs as this broth gets bold."
As meatballs roll in a jaunty parade,
You'll find happiness, that's homemade.

Broth of Reflection

A spoonful of life, all mixed up inside,
Like carrots and noodles, where secrets do hide.
The spices of fortune, a pinch of delight,
We stir up our dreams in the glow of the night.

Ladle out laughter, a glob of some fun,
With each slurp we ponder, what's come, what's undone.
Tomatoes of wisdom, zest for the soul,
The broth keeps us guessing, plays a funny role.

With garlic and humor, we simmer away,
Each bubble a giggle, the soup's grand display.
Beneath every surface, a story awaits,
In the pot of existence, laughter salivates.

So grab you a bowl, and don't hesitate,
Dive deep in the flavor, it's never too late.
For in every slosh, there's a jest to be found,
A broth full of nonsense, let joy abound!

Essence in the Cauldron

In a pot of delight, where chaos is brewed,
A pinch of the silly, a heap of good mood.
Carrots in costumes, peas in a dance,
Each flavor is singing, it's quite the romance.

With a splash of rejoicing, we stir and we grin,
The secrets of flavor, where the laughter begins.
Each noodle a whisper, each broth has its sway,
A savory riddle, come join for the play.

Ginger's a joker, with garlic a sage,
Each ingredient laughing, uncaged from their cage.
The essence, it coils in a steamy embrace,
A humorful journey, a whimsical chase.

So ladle it out, with a flick of your wrist,
In this cauldron of chaos, you don't want to miss.
For every warm bubble, tells tales from the heart,
In this broth of tomfoolery, we all get our start!

Beneath the Surface Flavors

Underneath the surface, where giggles reside,
The flavors are teasing, all jumbled inside.
Cabbage with stories, beans with a laugh,
A slosh of ruckus, the bowl's epitaph.

Each layer a quirk, each taste has a joke,
Beneath every spoonful, the punchlines invoke.
A creamy conundrum, a broth full of cheer,
With each taste you ponder, what's funny, my dear?

Oh, the secrets they stir, like the noodles of fate,
A swirl of confusion, the saucy debate.
With a sprinkle of laughter, and a dash of surprise,
The flavors unite, beneath giggling skies.

So come take a dip, bring your silliest face,
In this sea of absurd, we all find our place.
For deep in the broth, where the chuckles align,
You'll find all your answers, in pasta divine!

Secrets in the Simmer

In the simmering pot, where secrets are cooked,
A dash of the bizarre, and history's hooked.
The broth twirls and dances, with whimsy in tow,
Each bubble a chuckle, in the heating glow.

A splash of absurdity, as flavors collide,
With humor as spice, let's all take a ride.
The things that we ponder, they swirl and they sway,
In a cauldron of laughter, we melt the gray away.

Look closely, dear chef, at the soup's endless quest,
For the zany and saucy, are always the best.
Each sip is a riddle, each taste an embrace,
Where secrets are simmered, in this warming place.

So gather your friends, fill your bowls with good cheer,
Let's toast to the peculiar, let's savor the weird.
For in every thick drop, there's a ticklish surprise,
In the secrets of soup, where hilarity flies!

Viscosity of Thoughts

In a pot of ideas, they swirl and blend,
Curious flavors, where does it end?
A pinch of reason, a dash of dreams,
Stirred with laughter, or so it seems.

Thoughts bubble up like a hearty stew,
Nonsense at times, but oh, how true!
With every whiff, you have to ask,
Is this soup or a philosophical task?

A ladle of nonsense, a sprinkle of cheer,
Dipping into wisdom, sipping sincere.
But watch out now, it thickens fast,
Can't tell if it's genius or just a gas.

So grab a bowl, don't take it too serious,
Feeding on folly can be quite curious.
For in this broth of ideas and games,
Laughter is spiced in, and nothing's the same.

The Comfort of Familiar Flavors

In every kitchen, there's a secret taste,
A dash of comfort, never goes to waste.
Childhood memories in every bite,
Warmth in the broth that feels just right.

On cold winter nights, we gather 'round,
With slurps and giggles, we make our sound.
Frozen pizzas? Nah, pass the stew!
Swinging spoons like kids in the zoo.

The clatter of dishes, a poem unwritten,
Each swirl and twirl, the soup's a-fittin'.
Grandma's recipe, oh, what a find,
In every sip, old love is intertwined.

So here's to flavors that make us grin,
Scooping out joy, where do we begin?
For in this comfort, laughter brews,
Tasting the funny in family cues.

Broth as Metaphor

Some say life is like a pot, you see,
Boiling over with complexities.
Just toss in some veggies, let them stew,
Stirring the pot with a chuckle or two.

A sprinkle of chaos, a hint of role,
Broth holds secrets in a savory bowl.
It's not just food, it's life's grand play,
Sipping on riddles, come what may.

Wit mixed with wisdom, a swirl of jest,
Each taste of broth puts patience to test.
What's lurking beneath? A nugget of fun,
In this rich concoction, we're all one.

So bring out the ladle, let's all partake,
In this broth of laughter, for friendship's sake.
For every slurp holds a tale unique,
In the bubbling silence, hear all we speak.

The Harmony of Ingredients

In a bowl of mishmash, life finds a way,
Onion and garlic come out to play.
Tomatoes tumble into a mix so bright,
Creating a symphony that feels just right.

Celery's crunch, the zing of lime,
Tasting the chaos, it's simply sublime.
Each ingredient dancing, a humorous show,
Stirring up laughter, just letting it flow.

The melody of flavors, a comical tune,
Simmering slowly, like a jet ski on June.
With laughter as seasoning, we taste the delight,
Cooking up stories that sparkle with light.

So here's to the pot, the great mixing bowl,
Where every flavor plays a role.
In the kitchen of life, mix and repeat,
For harmony blossoms in laughter's sweet beat.

Celestial Cooking

Stirring up stars in a giant pot,
A ladle of laughter, oh what a lot!
Galaxy spices and a comet's zest,
In this kitchen, we're truly blessed!

Sizzle of suns, it's a cosmic feast,
Nebula noodles for the weary beast.
Taste of the moon and a sprinkle of mirth,
In this bizarre place, joy finds its birth!

Planets collide in a careless whirl,
While stardust bubbles and flavors unfurl.
Grab your forks, let the chaos ensue,
Each bite is a giggle, not one is askew!

Baked with a wink, fried with delight,
In this celestial dish, everything's right.
So let's raise our bowls to the skies above,
A universe served, steeped in love!

A Bowlful of Curiosity

What's in this broth? A curious blend,
A whisper of wonder, my taste buds send.
Dive in, my friend, let flavors unite,
Each spoonful a riddle, oh what a sight!

A splash of giggles and a dash of cheer,
Each sip tells stories we long to hear.
Pickles of puzzlement, marshmallows of joy,
In this brothy mix, we all can enjoy!

I swirled a question, then felt it pop,
What is reality in this bubbling shop?
With each little taste was a chortle and cheer,
Mysterious flavors that always endear!

So grab your bowl, let's delve into fun,
Each gulp a delight, no need to outrun.
Curiosity bubbles, come take a dip,
With soup as our muse, we'll dance and flip!

Hints of the Unseen

A whisk whispers secrets under a lid,
Each clink and clang, what could they bid?
In shadows of flavor, a melody plays,
Mysteries dwell in these culinary bays!

Spritz of the unknown, a pinch on the sly,
What's lurking beneath? I dare not deny.
A dollop of magic on the edge of dish,
Confirming that something is hidden—oh swish!

Peeking about, I catch magic's eye,
Hints of the unseen, I give it a try.
The broth seems to giggle, the veggies may dance,
What's lurking in here? Give it a chance!

So slurp with intent, and let spirits roam,
In this stew of the strange, we find our home.
Each spoonful a story, bold flavors tease,
In the hints of the unseen, we laugh with ease!

Sauces and Whispers

Sauces are gossiping, can you hear?
Spicy and mellow, they sing with cheer.
Ketchup confides, while mustard just laughs,
In this realm of flavor, it's more than just halves!

A drizzle of chat, a swirl of delight,
Each bottle a friend, oh such a sight!
They bubble and chatter, what stories they weave,
Magic in the kitchen, it's hard to believe!

Twirling the herbs, they join in the fray,
With aromas that beckon, "come join the play!"
A hint of shallots, a whisper of zest,
In this saucy affair, we are truly blessed!

So tip both your ladles and open your ears,
For sauces have tales that will bring you to cheers.
In the dance of the flavors, laughter prevails,
With each savory whisper, joy never fails!

www.ingramcontent.com/pod-product-compliance
Lightning Source LLC
Chambersburg PA
CBHW051656160426
43209CB00004B/921